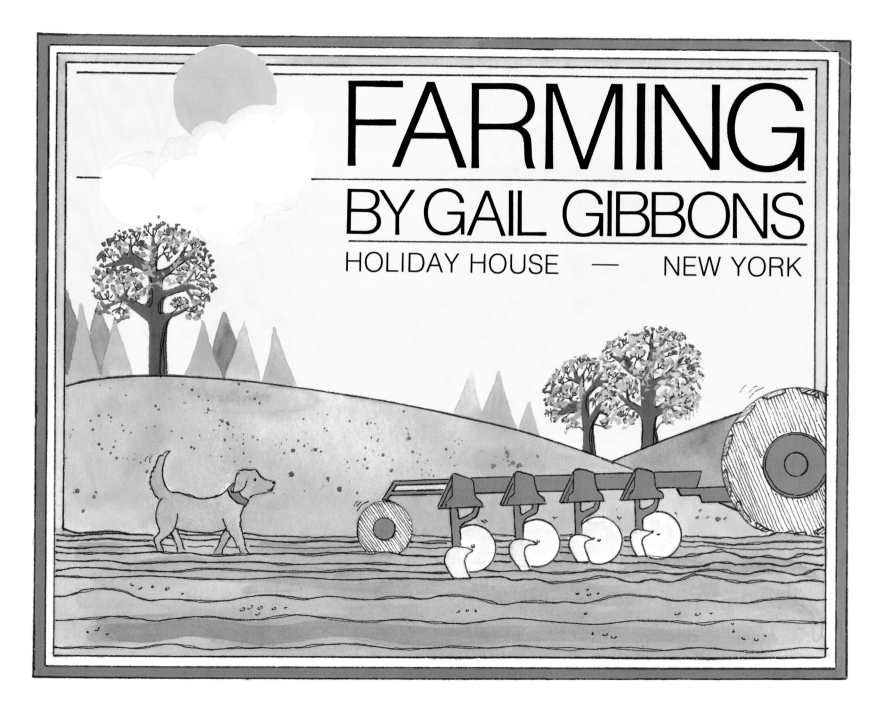

FARMING

BY GAIL GIBBONS

HOLIDAY HOUSE — NEW YORK

Special thanks to Maxine and Gregory Slack
of Corinth, VT; Rudy Martin of M&M Motors,
Montpelier, VT; J. S. Woodhouse Co., West
Springfield, MA; and Townline Equipment Sales,
Plainfield, NH

Library of Congress Cataloging-in-Publication Data

Gibbons, Gail.
Farming.

Summary: An introduction, in simple text and
illustrations, to farming and the work done on a
farm throughout the seasons.
1. Agriculture — Juvenile literature.   2. Farm life —
Juvenile literature.   3. Farms — Juvenile literature.
[1. Farms.   2. Farm life]   I. Title.
S519.G53   1988   630   87-21254
ISBN 0-8234-0682-2
ISBN 0-8234-0797-7 (pbk.)

ISBN-13: 978-0-8234-0682-1 (hardcase)
ISBN-13: 978-0-8234-0797-2 (paperback)

Farms are where vegetables, fruits and grains are grown and farm animals are raised.

Some farms are small . . .

others are big.

Most farms are owned by families.
They are busy places throughout the year.

Spring on the farm.

The days become longer.

Geese fly north.

Green leaves begin to appear on branches.

Baby chicks are brought to the chicken house.

chicken house

silo

barn

machine sh[ed]

farmhouse

There are baby lambs to check on in the barn.

The temperature climbs on the porch thermometer.

farm stand

Ice breaks up on the farm pond.

Spring flowers poke through the ground.

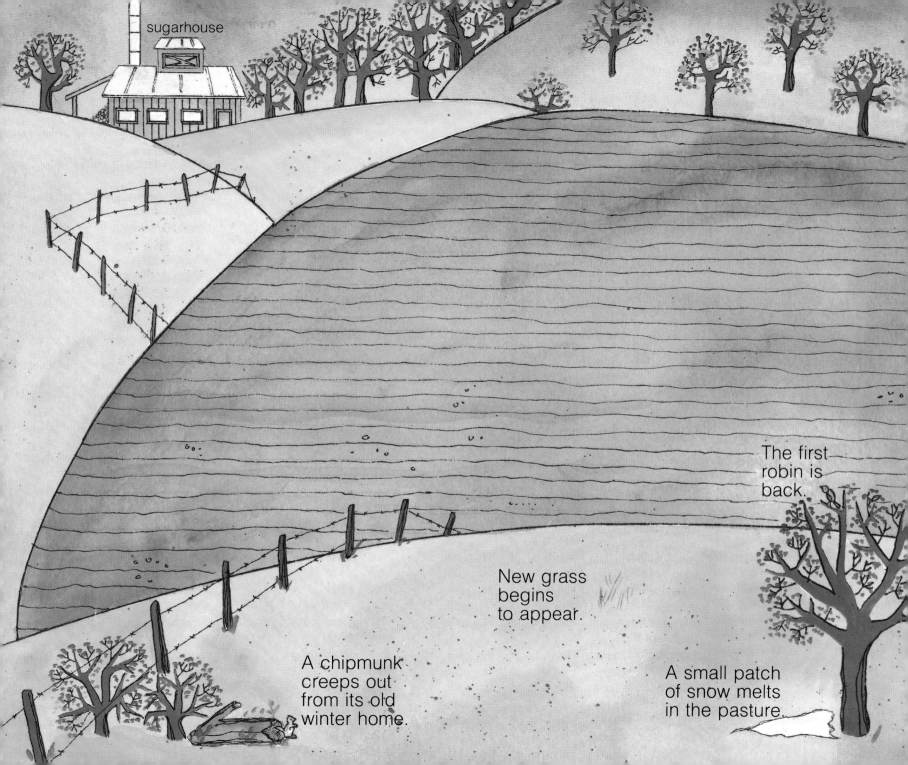

sugarhouse

The first robin is back.

New grass begins to appear.

A chipmunk creeps out from its old winter home.

A small patch of snow melts in the pasture.

Outside chores . . .

Horses and cows are put out to pasture.

The vegetable garden is planted.

The maple syrup season has just ended.

Water is lugged to the chicken house.

Fields are fertilized . . .

fertilizer spreader

plowed . . .

The plow turns over the soil.

harrowed . . .

The harrows make the ground smooth.

and planted.

The planter plants the seeds.

and inside chores.

The stalls
are always
being cleaned.

The new
baby chicks
need constant
care.

There are new farm babies.

The cows are milked in the morning and in the evening.

Summer on the farm.

It is hot.

beehives

Bees collect nectar from flowers to make honey.

The garden is hoed.

Vegetables grow in the garden.

Time to go swimming!

Flowers bloom.

The hay
grows tall.

The corn
grows tall.

The baby
animals are
bigger now.

Cows munch
grass.

Outside chores . . .

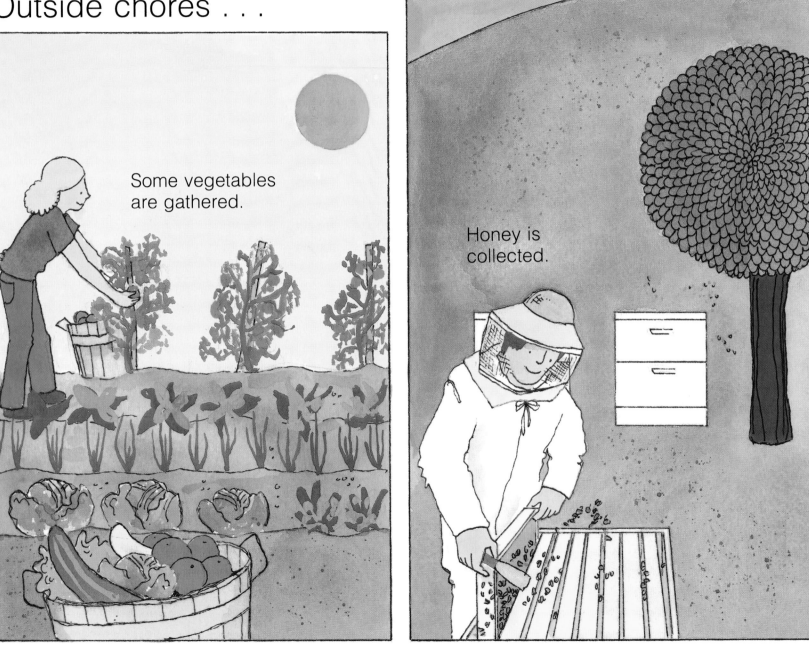

Some vegetables
are gathered.

Honey is
collected.

The hay is mowed . . .

The mower cuts the hay.

tedded. . . .

The tedder spreads the hay to dry.

raked . . .

The raker puts the hay in rows.

and baled.

The baler bales the hay.

and inside chores.

Vegetables are
canned or frozen.

canning jars

Eggs are
collected
each day
of the year.

The vet
gives a
calf a
checkup.

The cows are milked twice a day every day of the year.

The hay is put in the hayloft.

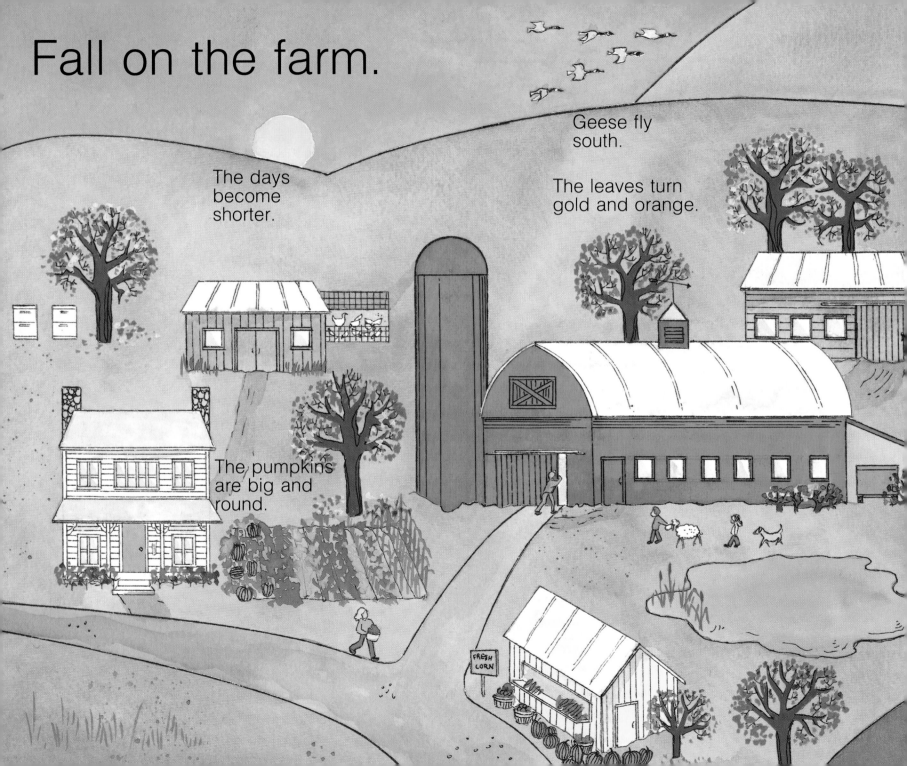

Fall on the farm.

Geese fly south.

The days become shorter.

The leaves turn gold and orange.

The pumpkins are big and round.

FRESH CORN

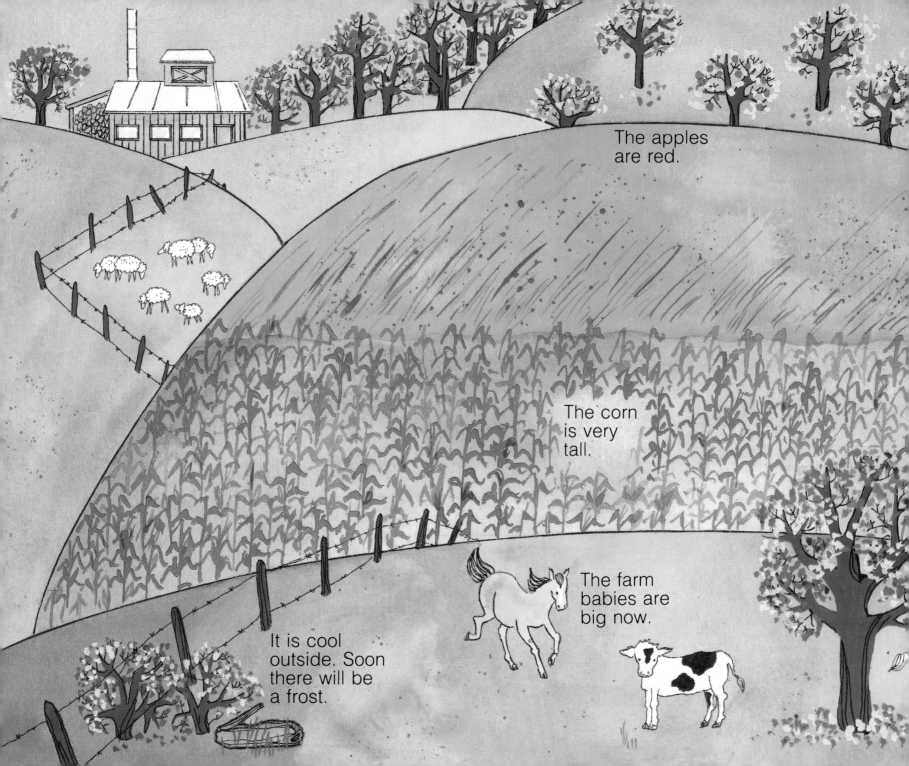

The apples are red.

The corn is very tall.

The farm babies are big now.

It is cool outside. Soon there will be a frost.

Outside chores . . .

After morning chores, it's time to go to school.

Eggs are packed for delivery.

At the end of the growing season, all fruits and vegetables are harvested.

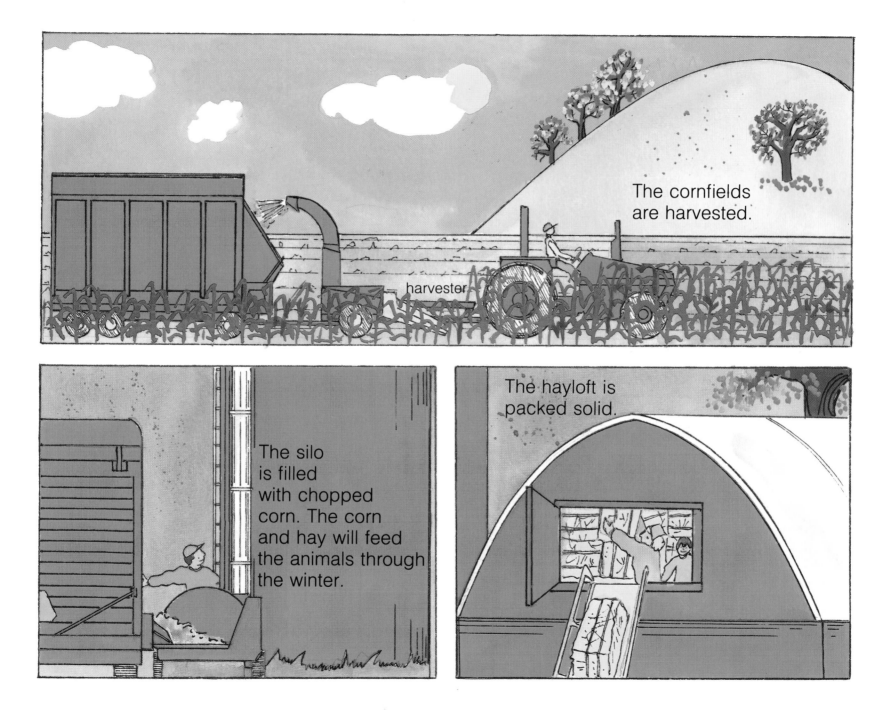

The cornfields are harvested.

harvester

The silo is filled with chopped corn. The corn and hay will feed the animals through the winter.

The hayloft is packed solid.

and inside chores.

Bushels of apples have been put in the farmstand.

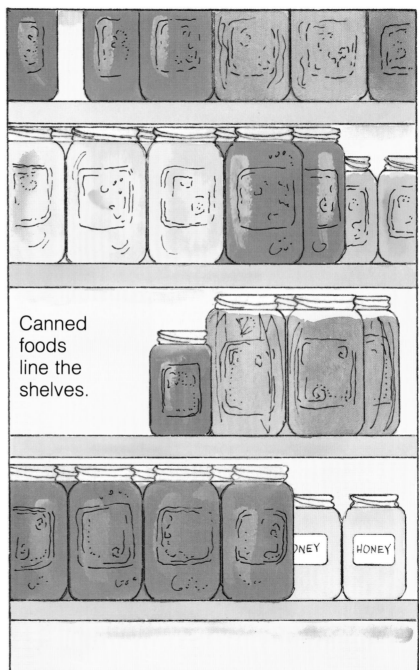

Canned foods line the shelves.

Some animals are going to market to be sold.

The cows' milk is sold to a dairy throughout the year.

Winter on the farm.

The days
are short.

Footprints
lead to
the barn.

Ice is on
the pond.

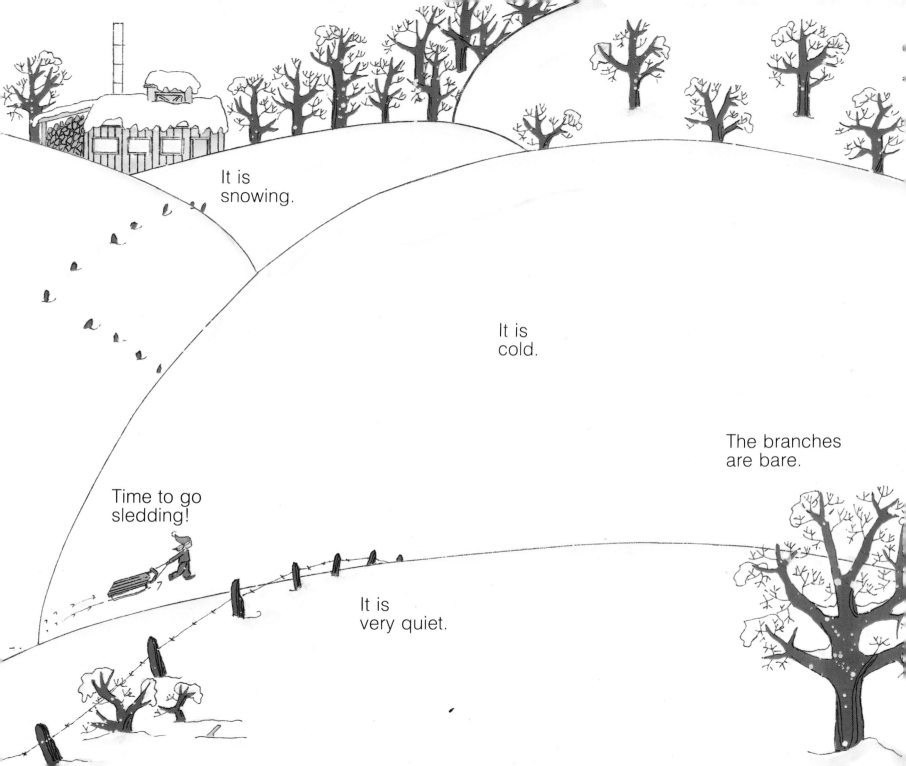

It is
snowing.

It is
cold.

The branches
are bare.

Time to go
sledding!

It is
very quiet.

Outside chores . . .

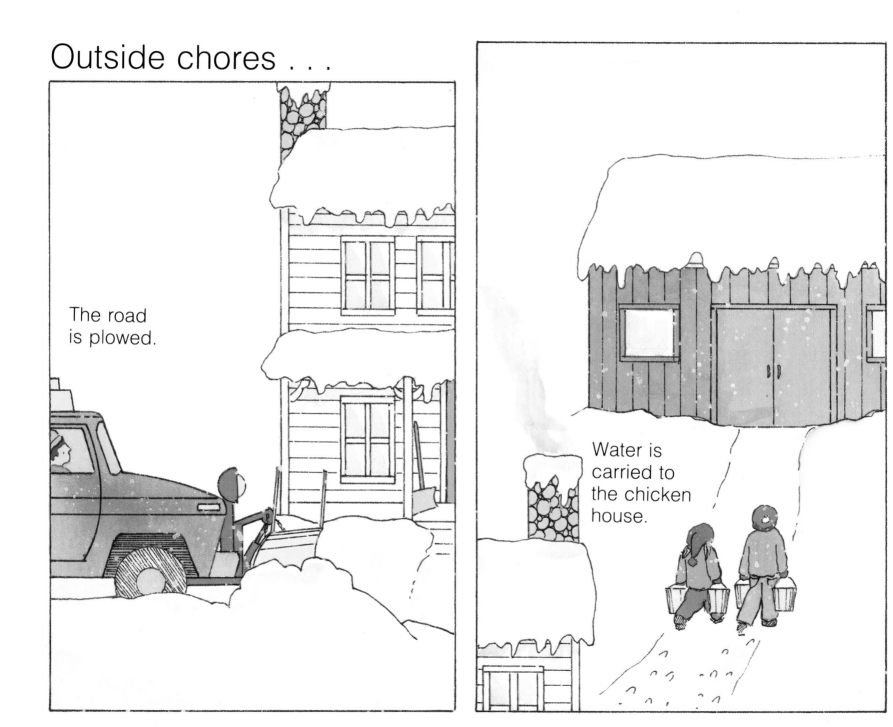

The road
is plowed.

Water is
carried to
the chicken
house.

and inside chores.

Farm machinery is repaired and cleaned.

The cows are milked.

There is plenty of hay and grain to eat.

All the animals are inside for the cold winter.

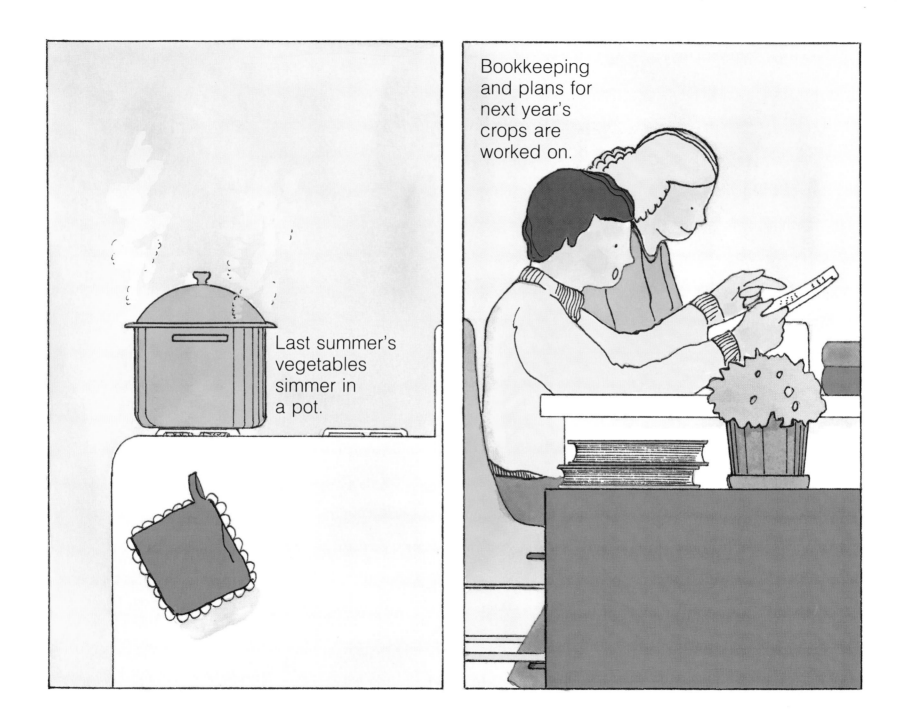

Last summer's
vegetables
simmer in
a pot.

Bookkeeping
and plans for
next year's
crops are
worked on.

In winter everyone goes to bed early.

Soon spring will come again.

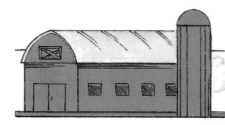

KINDS OF FARMING

Most farms are specialized. They produce one or two main crops or kinds of farm animals.

DAIRY FARMS

Dairy farms raise dairy cows for their milk. The milk is sold to dairies where it is processed and packaged.

EGG AND POULTRY FARMS

Egg farms raise chickens to lay eggs. Poultry farms raise chickens for their meat.

GRAIN FARMS

Grain farms grow grain for making bread and cereals
and other foods.
Some grains are grown for animals, too.

FRUIT FARMS

Fruit farms grow apples, peaches, oranges and
other fruits for people to eat.

VEGETABLE FARMS

Vegetable farms grow beans, lettuce, carrots and other vegetables. They are sent to market and stores to be sold.

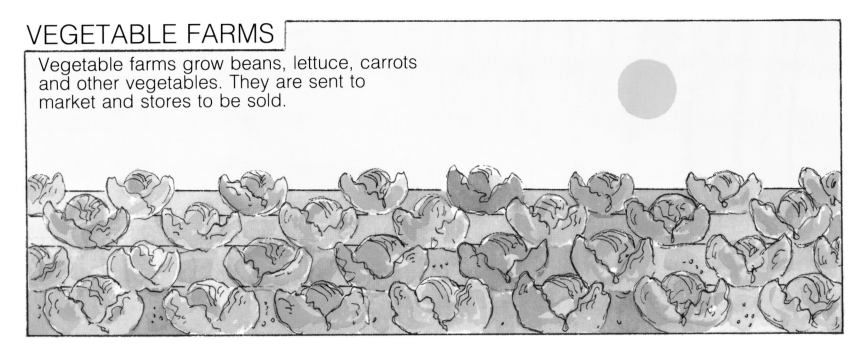

CATTLE FARMS AND RANCHES

Beef cattle, pigs and other animals are raised for their meat.